optical
illusions

optical illusions

Over 70 of the most **mind-bending,** brain-melting, **illusions** ever **invented**

Compiled by Tim Leng

DOG 'n' BONE

Published in 2013 by Dog 'n' Bone Books
An imprint of Ryland Peters & Small Ltd
20–21 Jockey's Fields
London WC1R 4BW
519 Broadway, 5th Floor
New York, NY 10012

www.rylandpeters.com

10 9 8 7 6 5 4 3 2 1

A CIP catalog record for this book is available from the Library of Congress and the British Library.

ISBN: 978 1 909313 08 8

Printed in China

Text and image compilation: Tim Leng
Editor: Pete Jorgensen
Designer: Ashley Western
Picture credits: see page 128

For digital editions, visit www.cicobooks.com/apps.php

contents

Introduction 7

THE ILLUSIONS 9

Spirals 11
Age Before Beauty? 12
Four Legs Good? 14
Rabbit or Duck 15
Native Eskimo 16
Face to Face 17
Eiffel Tower 19
Kinetic Colors 20
Sun Terrace 21
Blow Me Down 23
Fire Escape 24
Skulls 27
Blowing Bubbles 28
Baubles 31
Necker Cube 32
The Worst Commute 33
Covent Garden 34
Cloud Spotting 36
The Right Profile 37
Funny Business 39
Color Waves 40
Hollywood Sunset 43
Adelson Shadow Checker 44
Bulging Buddha 46
Vibrating Sun 47
3D Garden 48
City Lights 50
Smoke Alarm 51
Barcode Cat 52
In the Shadows 55
Giant Pancakes 56
How to Fill a Hole 57
Caterpiller Race 58
Hole In the Mall 61
Revolution 62
Hidden Anubis 64
Hand Writing 66
Inky Fingers 67
Zig Zag 69
A Life-sized Photograph 70
Haunted Head 71
Front Runners 73
Invisible Triangle 74
The Right Angle 75
Hook, Line, and Sinker 77
Impossible Production Line 78
Vortex 81
Down of the Upside 82
Starfloat 84
Not Everything is Black and White 87
Fighter Jet 88
Square Eyes 90
Keep Still! 93
Taking the Edge Off 94
Bugs in a Box 95
Giddy Up! 97
Twister 98
Fraser Spiral 101
Coffee Break 102
Up, Down, Left, Right 105
Hand Out 106
Small Circles 108
Star Fall 109
Wavy Checkerboard 110
Let's Get This Straight 113
Dog Gone Fun 115
Art Imitates Life 116
No Escape 117
Reverse Opposites 118
Tunnel Vision 121
Wood Splitter 122
Tangled Star 124
Shape Shifting 125
Play Time 127

Picture Credits 128

Introduction

Optical illusions are funny old things. You can spend hours looking at them and see one thing, only to turn away then glance back a few seconds later to see something completely different. It's little wonder that many of us have long been fascinated by them in all their many forms and guises. For example, I can distinctly remember the first stereogram image (y'know, the sort of things where there's a picture hidden within a picture) I ever saw: I was a little kid, and it was hanging in a shop window. After intently staring at the picture for what seemed like forever, I suddenly found myself confronted with a massive T-Rex looming out of the frame, all sharp teeth and tiny arms. It was terrifying and brilliant in equal measure, and I was addicted (to stereograms, I mean, not T-Rexes!).

When I was first asked to compile this book I immediately knew that there were some classics of the genre that it would simply be rude not to include—although we've breathed new life into them thanks to the talents of one of the many wonderful artists who have contributed to the book—but what to feature beyond those defining images? To answer that, we trawled the globe looking for some of the best, most original, most awe-inspiring optical illusions we could find. The sort of illusions that would linger in your mind long after you first looked at them. Ones that you'd look back at time and again, purely to try and work out exactly how it does what it does.

What follows, then, is a collection of the best of the very best, from the aforementioned classics to street art, stereograms to after images—there's something here for everyone. Some will astound you, some will confuse you, and some will simply mess with your mind.

Enjoy.

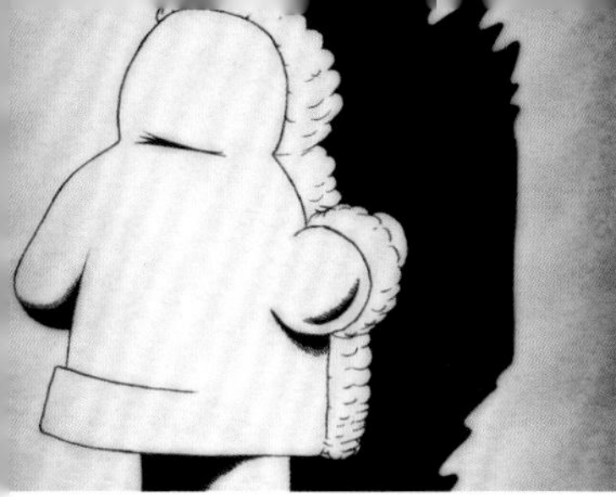
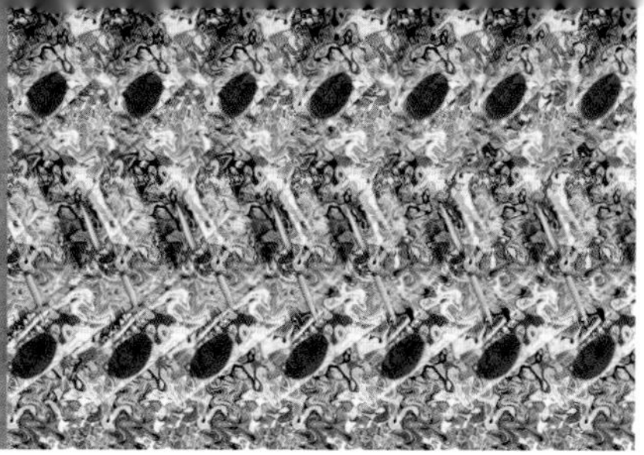

The Illusions

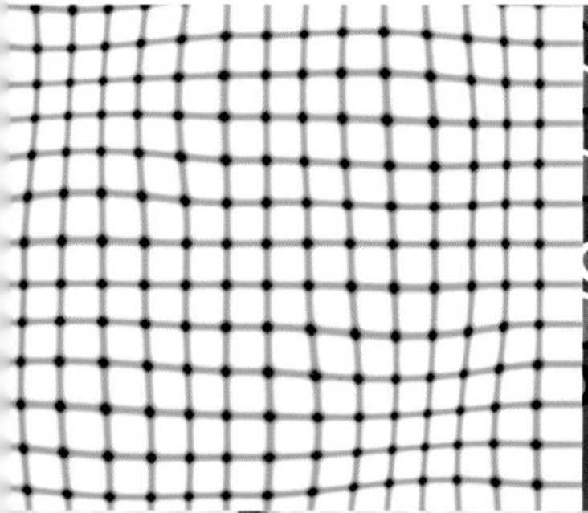

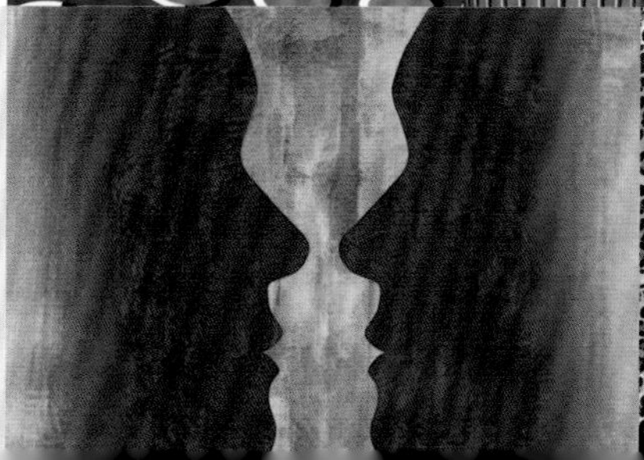
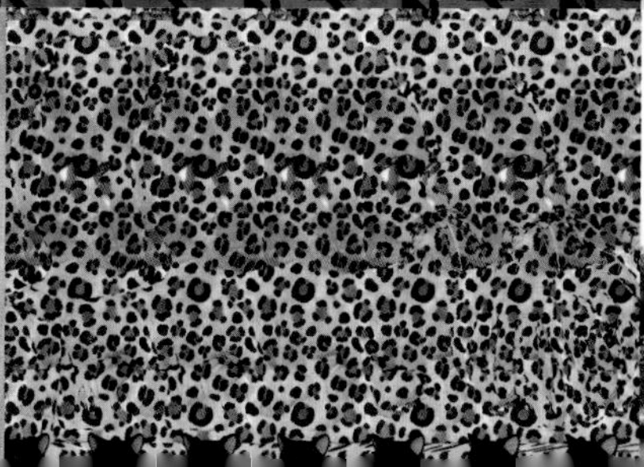

Spirals

Move **your eyes around** the image and **watch the circles** rotate.

Age Before **Beauty?**

What do **you** see—
a beautiful young **lady**
or an **old woman?**

Four **Legs** Good?

How many legs does this elephant **have?**

One picture, two totally different animals. What do you see—a duck or a rabbit?

Rabbit or Duck

Native

Eskimo

Do you see a **Native** American **warrior** or an Eskimo **braving the cold?**

Face **to** Face

This classic illustration will **no doubt be familiar** to many. Is it a chalice **or two faces staring** at each other?

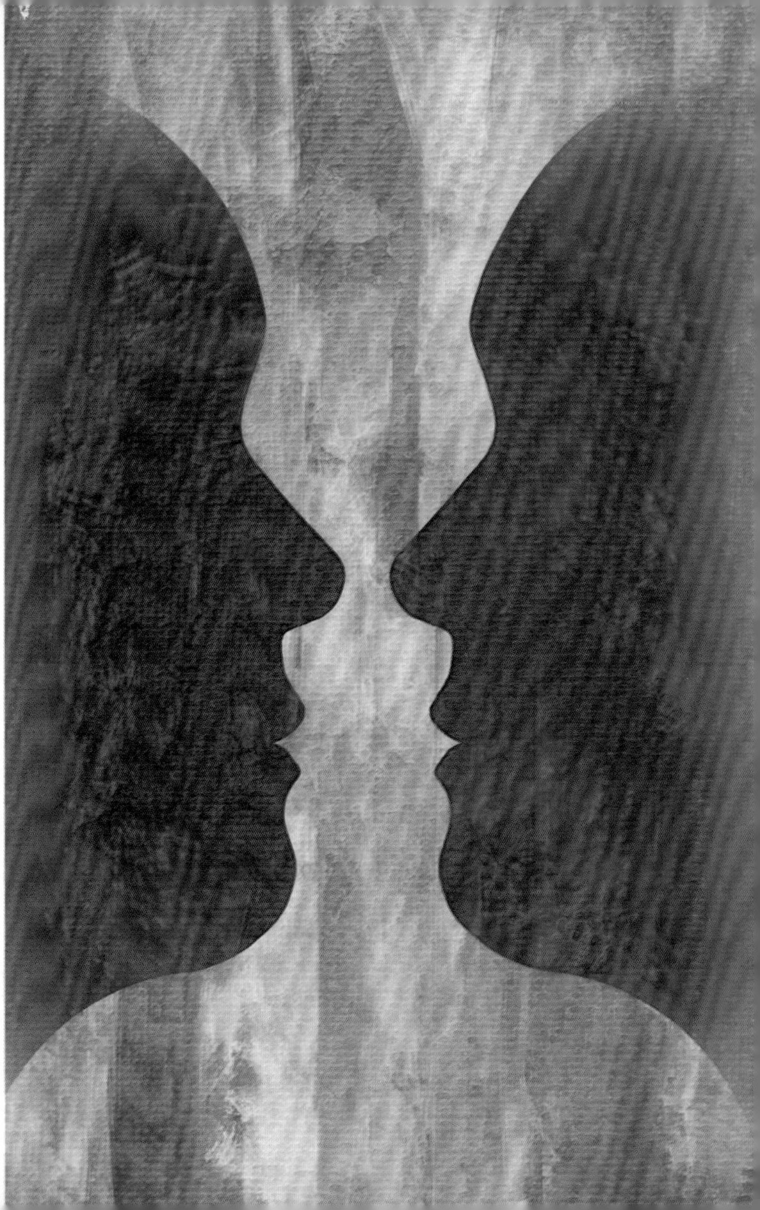

Eiffel Tower

A rain-drenched photograph taken beneath the Eiffel Tower, but can you see the face staring at you?

Kinetic **Colors**

Everything in this **image moves!**

Sun Terrace

Are these builders working on the roof or the floor?

Blow Me Down

A run-down **house** filled with balloons, or a **beautifully** realized **optical illusion?**

Fire Escape

A typical **New York City fire escape... but which way is up** and which way **is down?**

Skulls

From afar you might **be forgiven** for thinking these **two** paintings just show **human skulls,** but look closer **and you'll see there's** far more **to them than meets** the eye...

Blowing **Bubbles**

Place the page very close to your **eyes, so you can't focus.**

Slowly move the image away from **your eyes**

but don't focus on the image.

It will start to appear **in 3D**.

Baubles

Watch **these baubles come** to **life** as you move **your eyes around** the page!

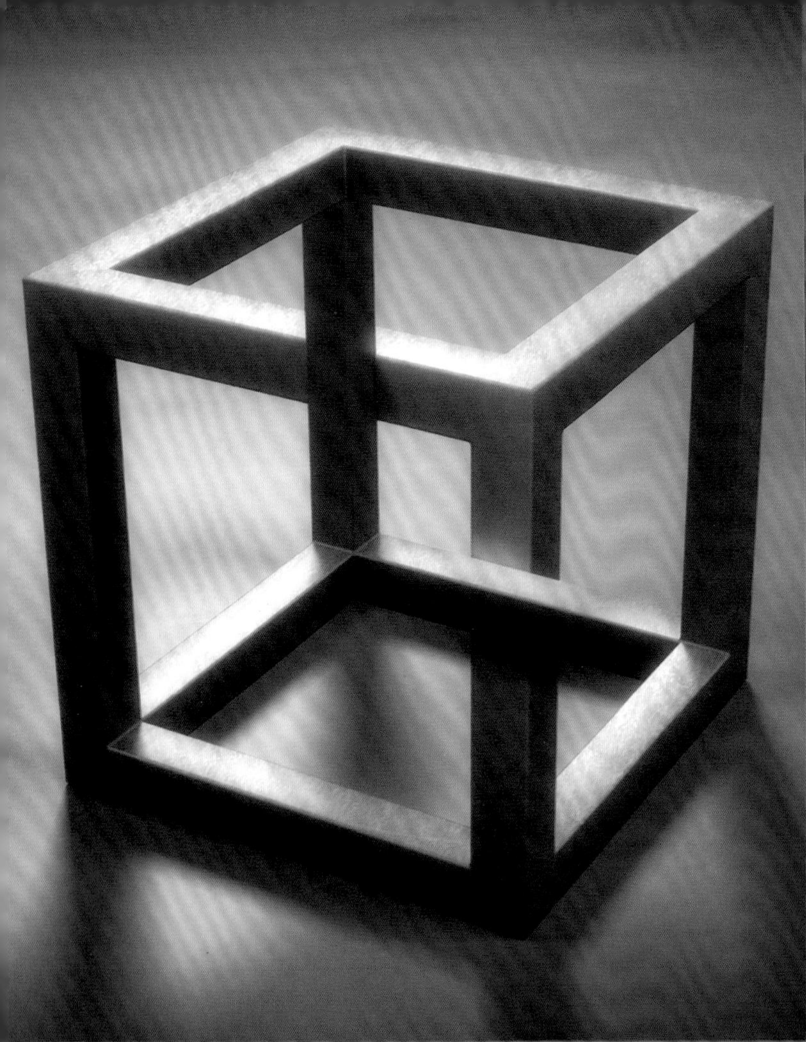

Necker Cube

A seemingly impossible cube where it's difficult to see what's at the front and what's at the back.

The Worst Commute

How will this man ever get to work?

Covent Garden

Avoid the crowds at one of London's busiest tourist hotspots by teetering above it on towering stilts!

GREAT
英国
知识
是
GREAT
GREAT
BRITAIN YOU'RE INVITED
COVENT GARDEN
GREAT
GREAT

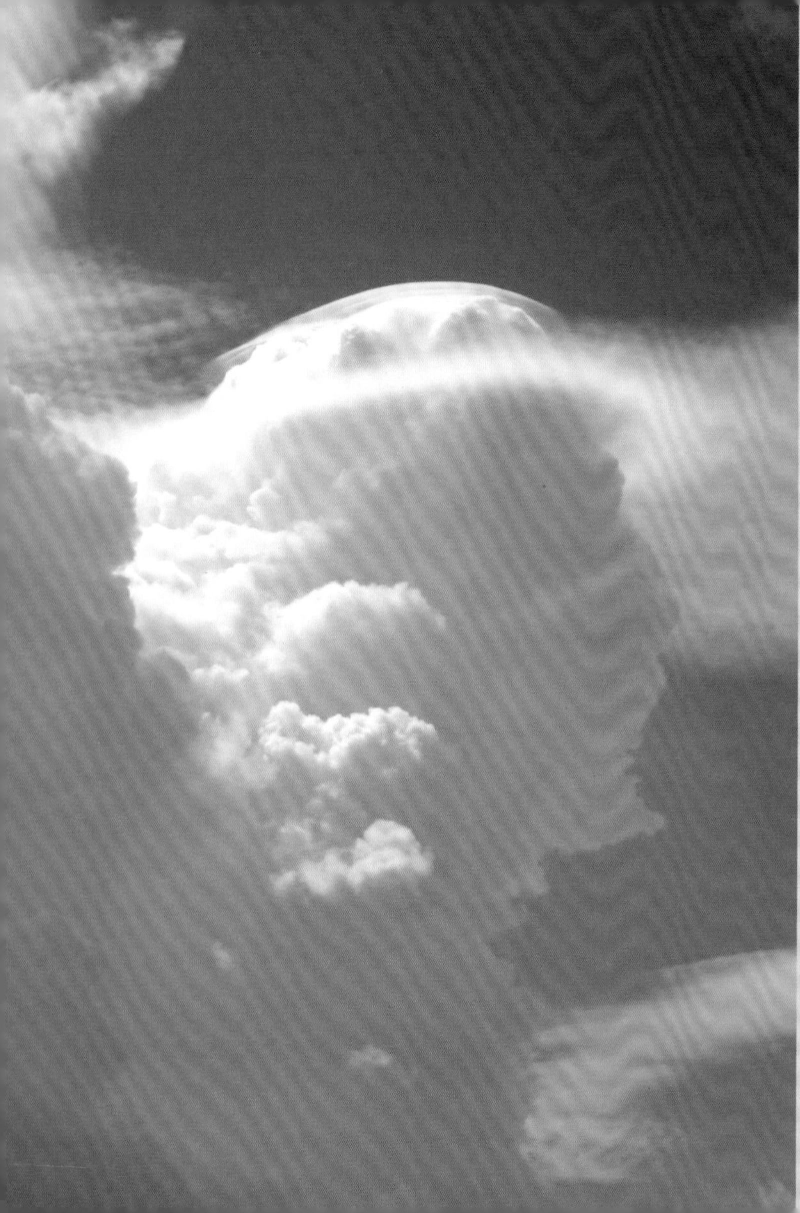

Cloud Spotting

Can you see the face in the clouds?

The **Right** Profile

Is this man looking at **you** or **away** from you?

Funny Business

When your office **block** has gone **as high** as it can, **the only way is** down.

Color Waves

One of the trippiest optical illusions you'll ever see, man...

Hollywood Sunset

Look carefully at the setting sun—do you see **the face** of legendary Hollywood **icon** Marilyn Monroe?

Adelson Shadow **Checker**

Square A **appears** darker than **Square B**… but would **you believe they're actually the** same color?

A
B
A
B

Bulging Buddha

Focus on the **Buddha** in the center of the page **and watch everything around him** ripple into **motion.**

Vibrating Sun

Watch **how this starburst** pattern **leaps off the page as you** stare **at it.**

3d Garden

Hold the page so close to your face that you can't focus on the image. As you slowly move it away from you, without focusing, you'll find that the grass and clouds begin to appear in 3D.

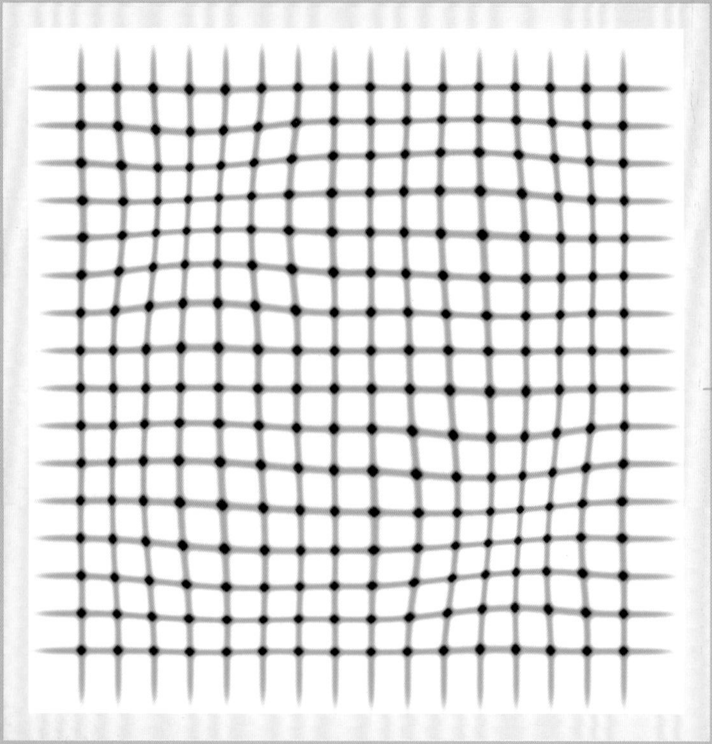

City Lights

If you try to focus on the **white dots where** the lines **intersect** you'll soon **discover**... there are **no** white dots!

Smoke Alarm

Don't **be** frightened **when you** see the face appear **in this cloud** of smoke.

Barcode Cat

Shake your **head**
from side to side.
What do you **see**
emerging from the lines?

In the Shadows

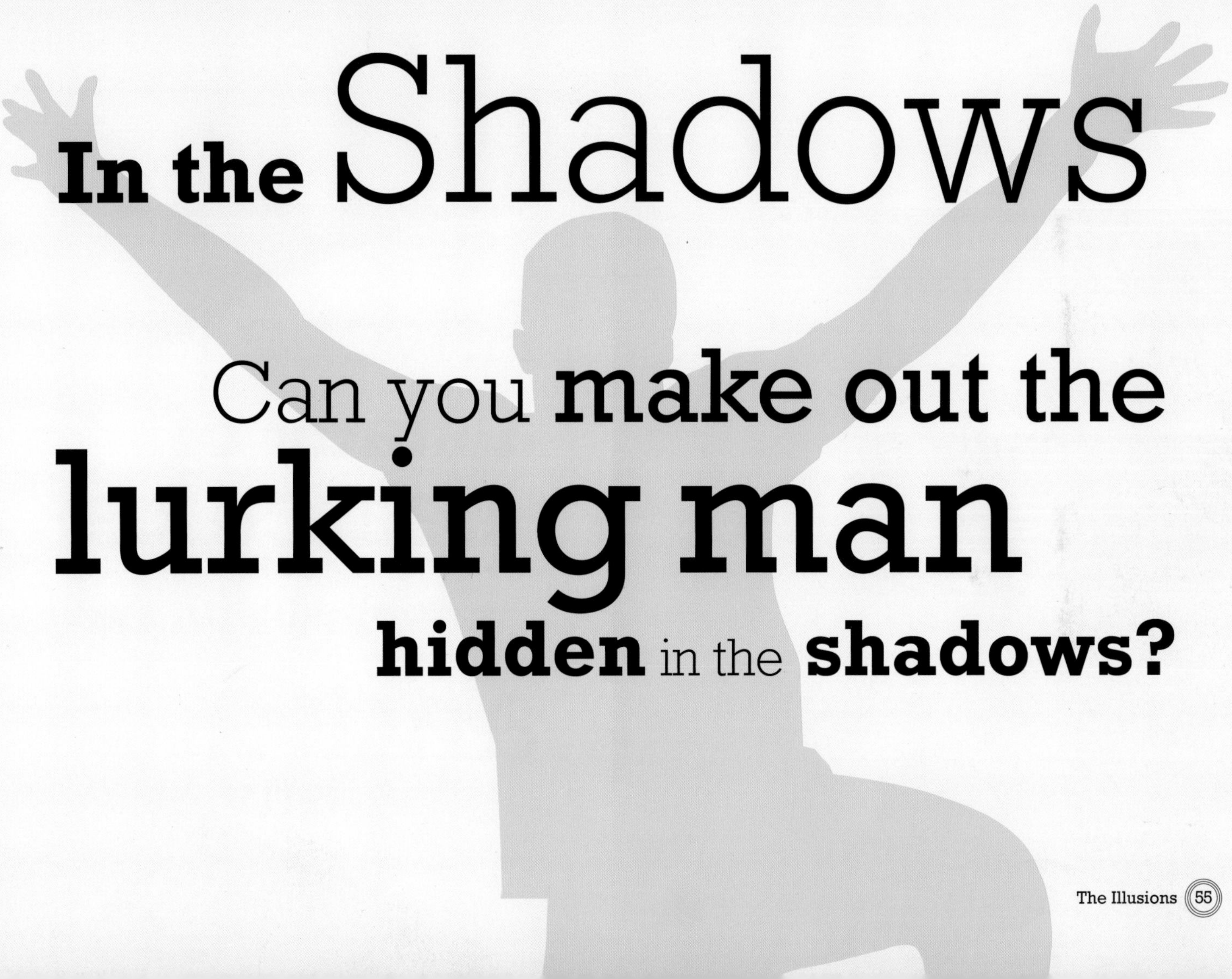

Can you make out the lurking man hidden in the shadows?

Giant Pancakes

Anyone fancy
a stack of
pancakes
topped with syrup
and...
a tiny lady?

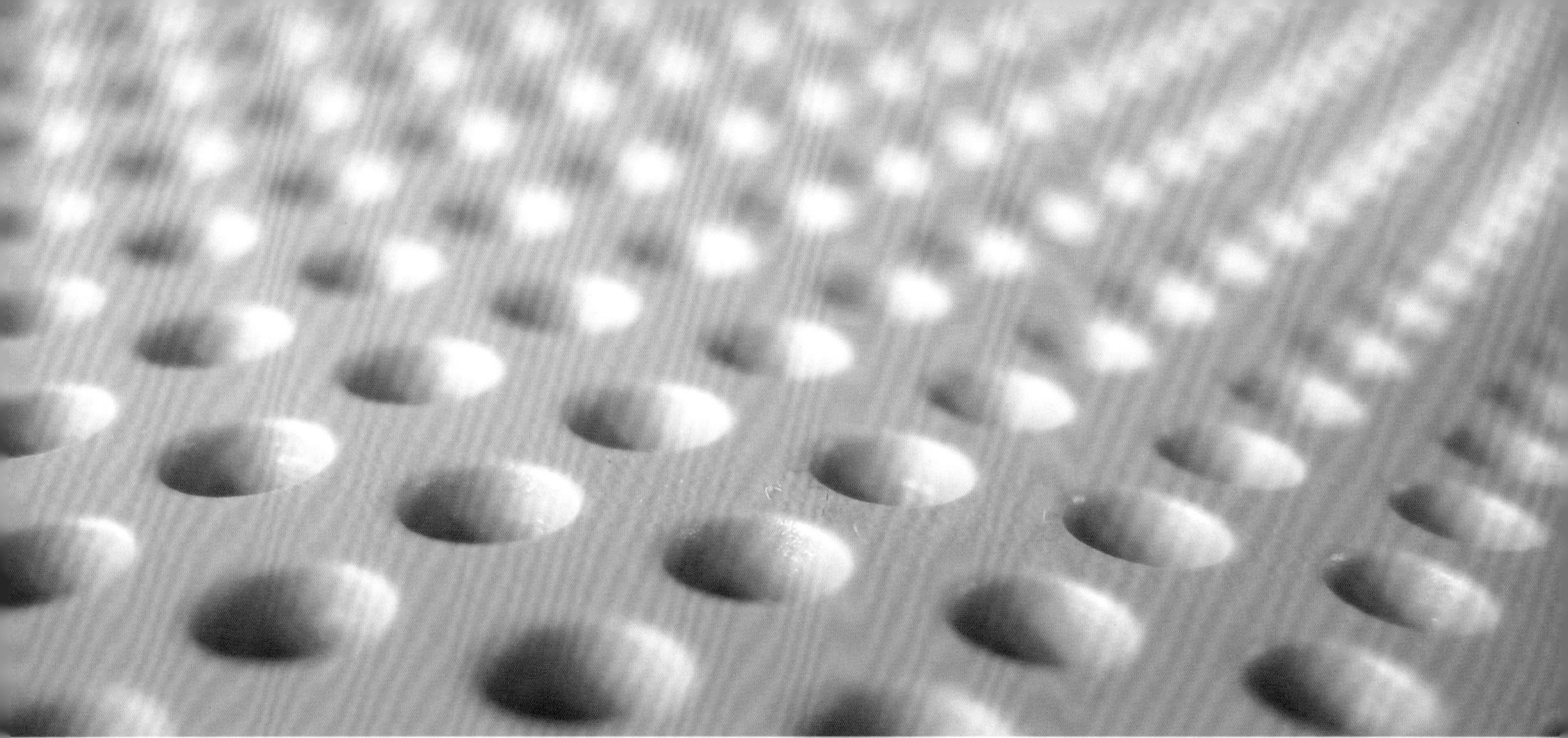

How to Fill a Hole

Are these shapes above the ground or below it?

Caterpillar Race

Pick a caterpillar!

Will **your chosen**

competitor make it to the **side** of the page **before** the **others?**

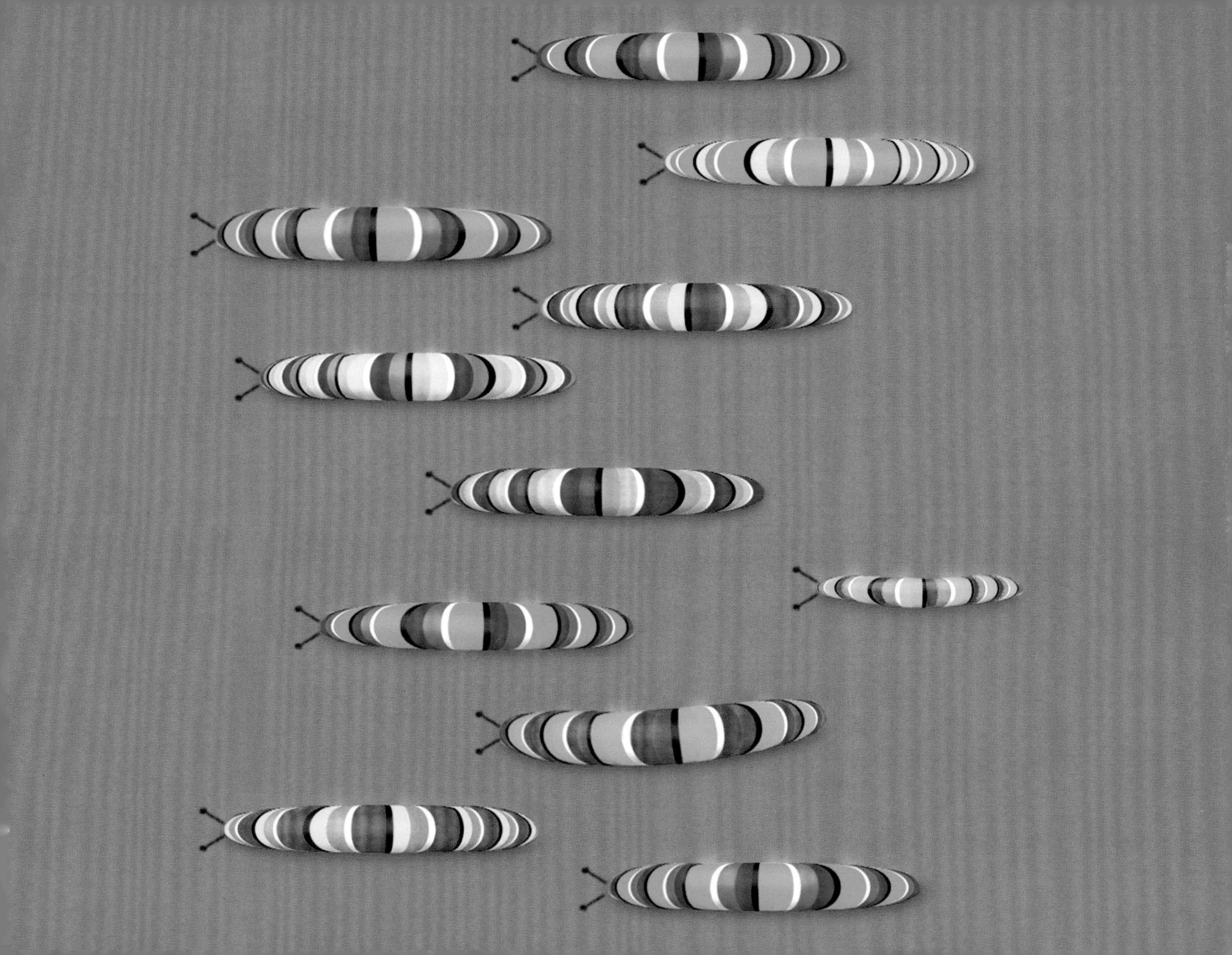

PERRY
SPORT + OUTDOOR
ROXY

Hole In the Mall

A regular shopping center is transformed by some hand-painted ancient architectural additions.

Revolution

Are the shapes in this circle spinning clockwise or counterclockwise?

Hidden Anubis

Following **the instructions** on page 28, **can you see the ancient Egyptian god Anubis?**

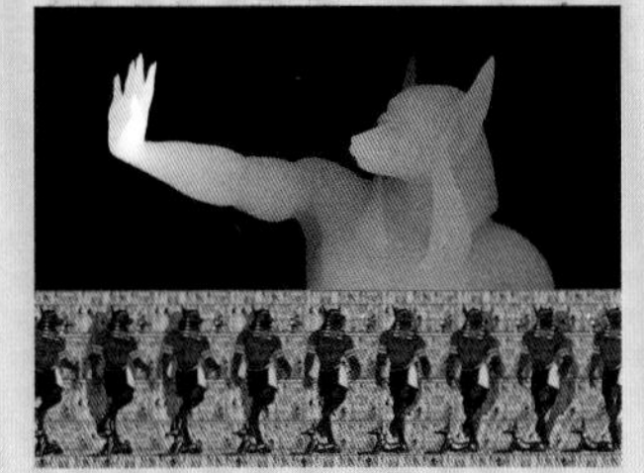

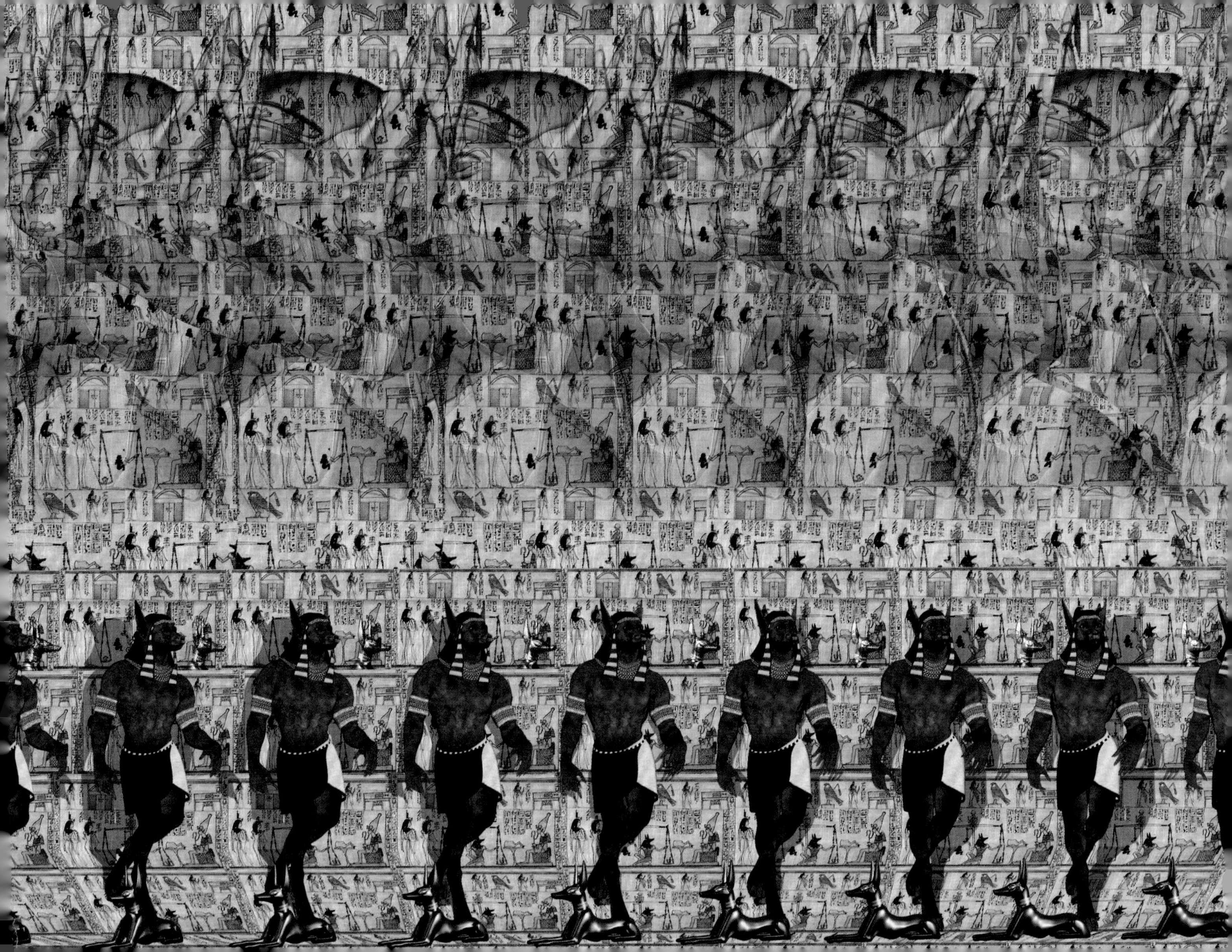

Hand Writing

Where does the **hand** end and **the pen** begin?

Inky Fingers

A pot full of an artist's tools, or is there something else at hand here?

Zig **Zag**

Focus on the **center** of the image and watch the **pattern** start to move.

A Life-sized Photograph

An old man and an oversized camera, but only one is real while the other is a trick of perspective.

Haunted Head

Focus on the X in the **middle** of this **image** for 30 **seconds, then turn to look at** a blank wall… **Are you haunted by the** floating skull?

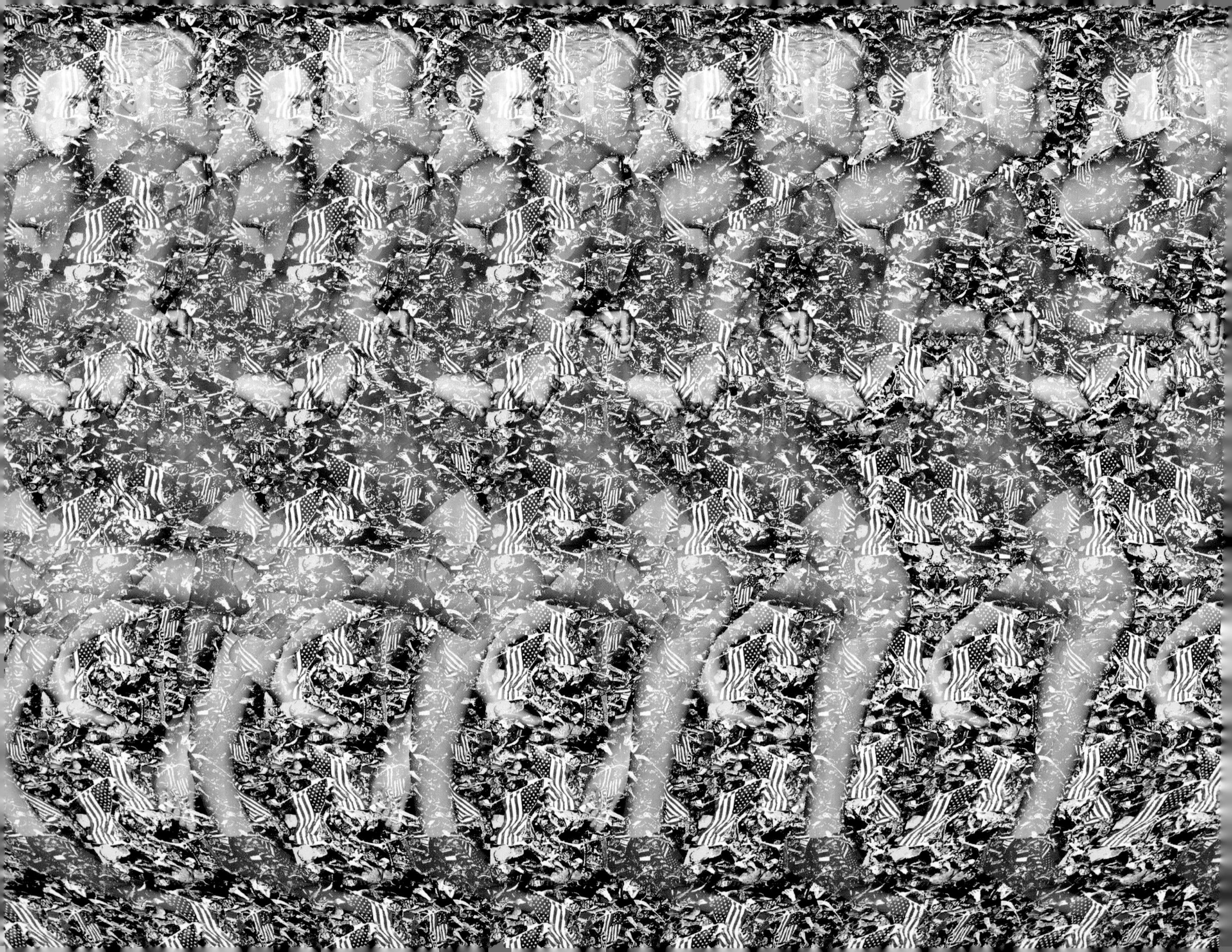

Front Runners

Who is **going to**

win the race?

Use the instructions **on page 28**

to find out.

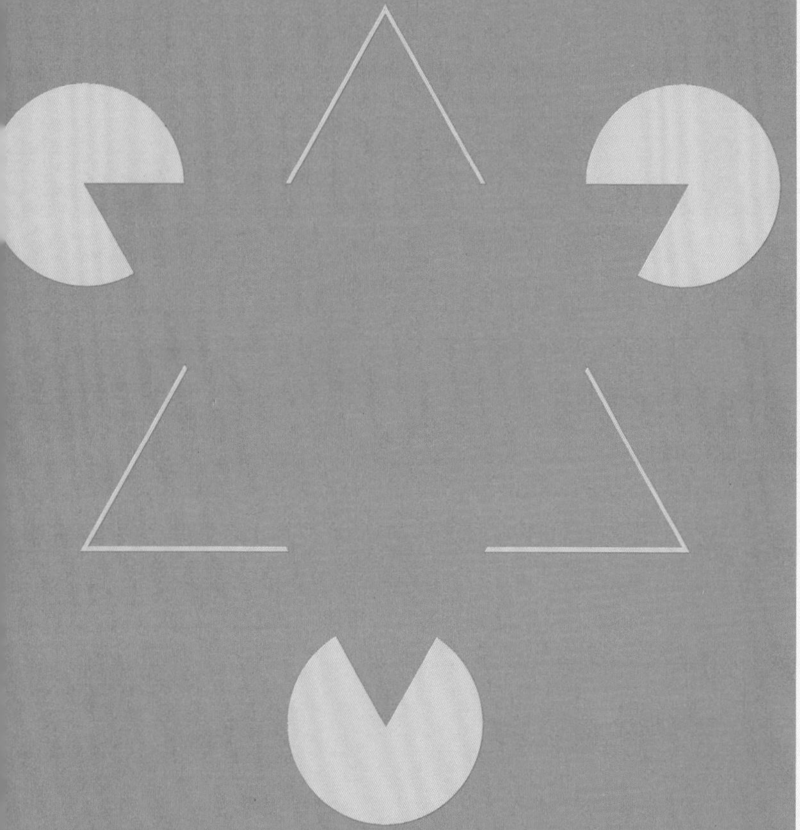

Invisible **Triangle**

This simple illusion **tricks** your mind **into seeing** a triangle where none actually **exists!**

The Right Angle

While these lines might look like they're angled, would you believe they're actually parallel to one another?

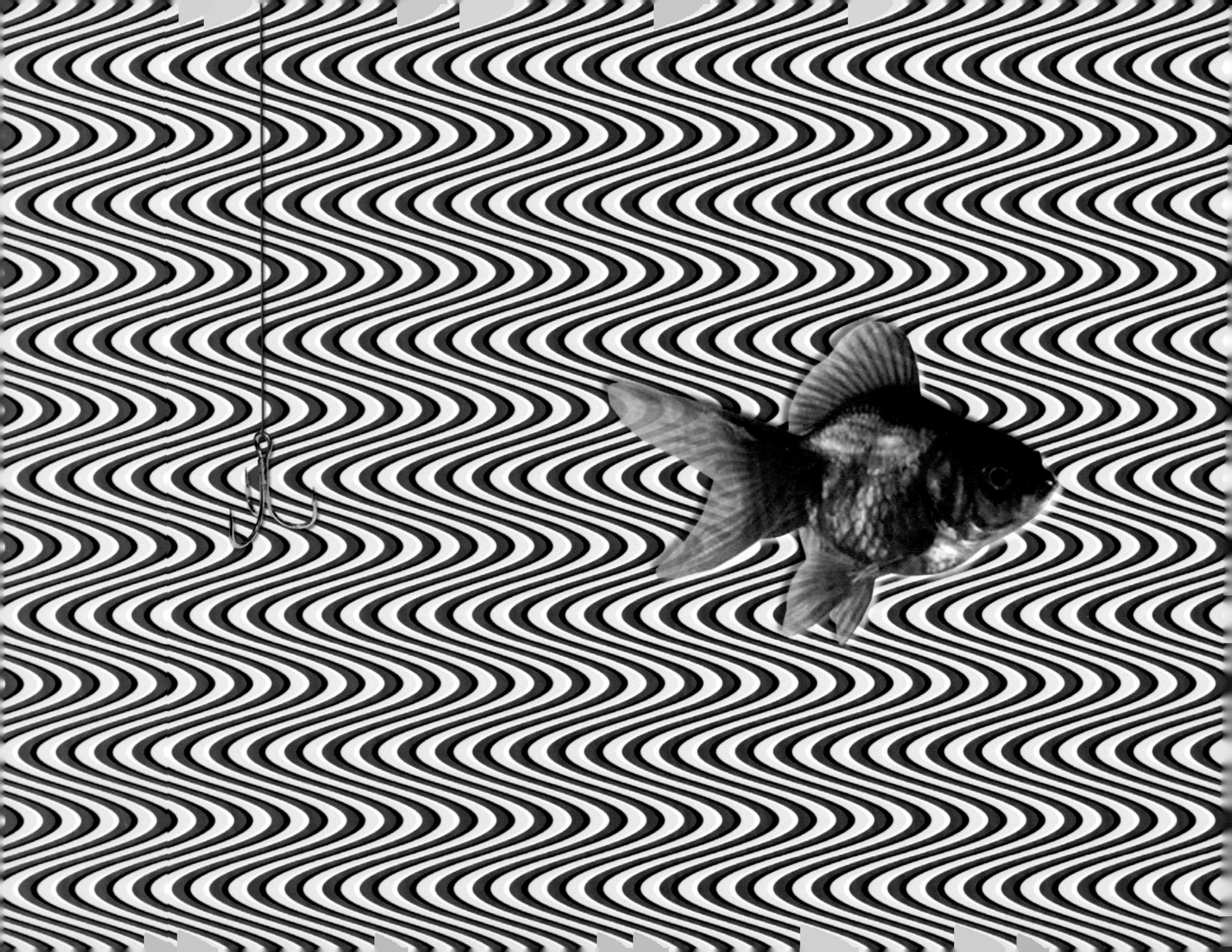

Hook, **Line, and Sinker**

This fish is fighting

to get away

but is the current

of the waves **too strong?**

Impossible Production Line

These factory workers can't work out where to start and when to stop.

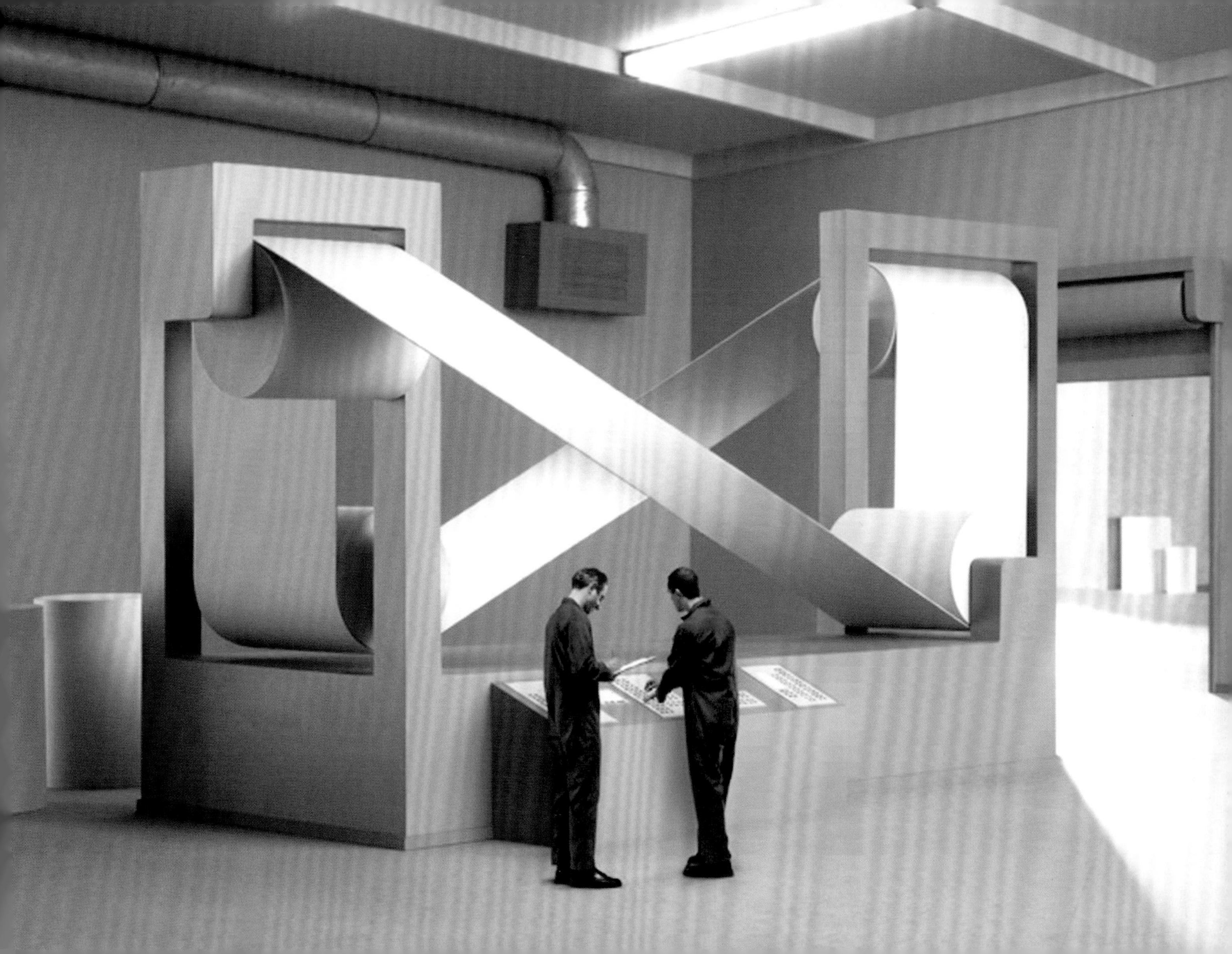

Vortex

Don't get sucked in as this illusion spins round and round.

Down of the Upside

Two men **on a bridge remain separated** by the distance and an unnatural **twist in reality.**

Starfloat

Focus on the floating star in the middle of the page and watch as it moves counterclockwise to the background.

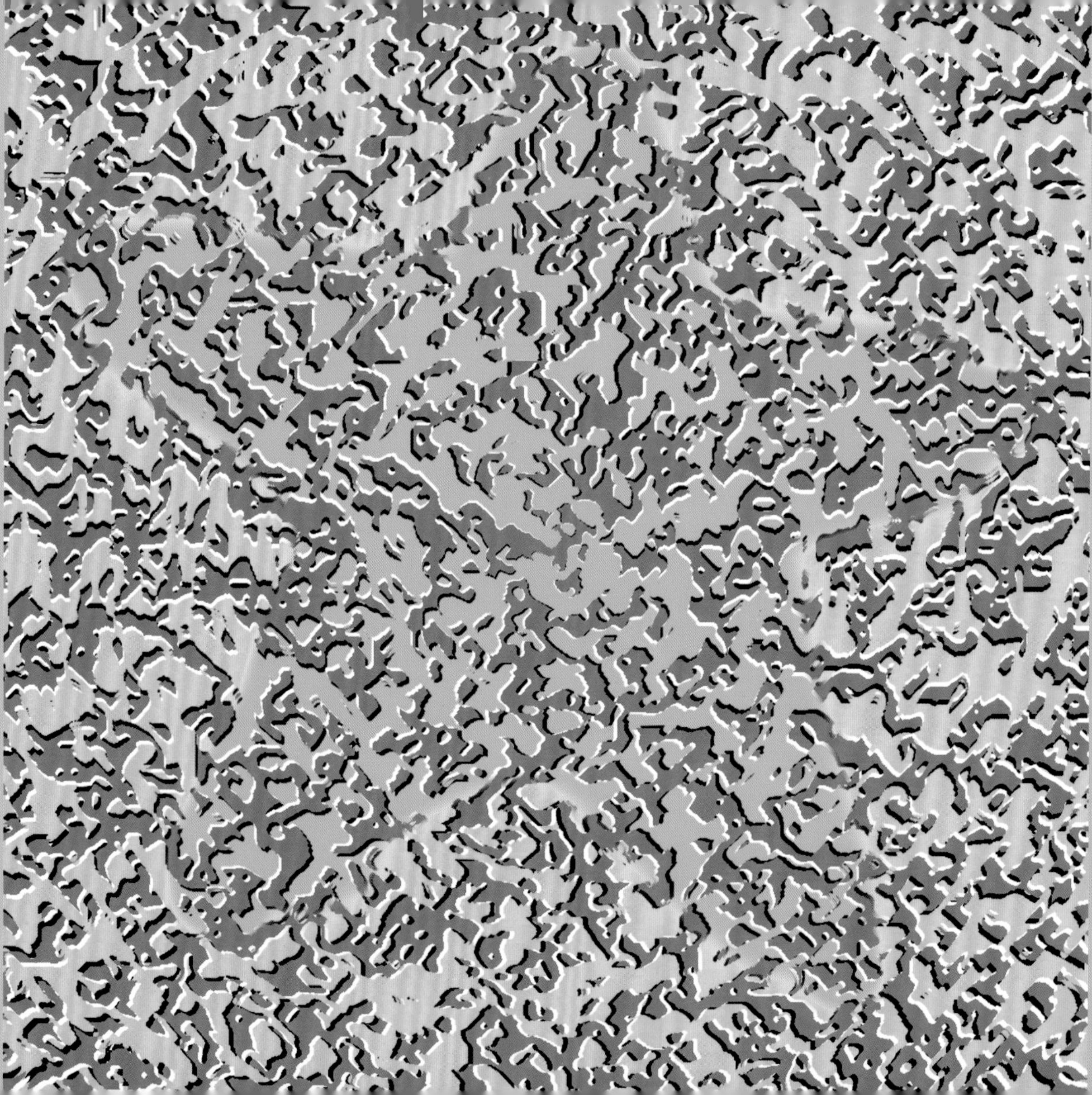

Not **Everything** is
Black **and White**

If these images are **flat then**
why do they look
like they **keep moving?**

Fighter Jet

If you follow the tips on page 28, this aircraft is plain to see.

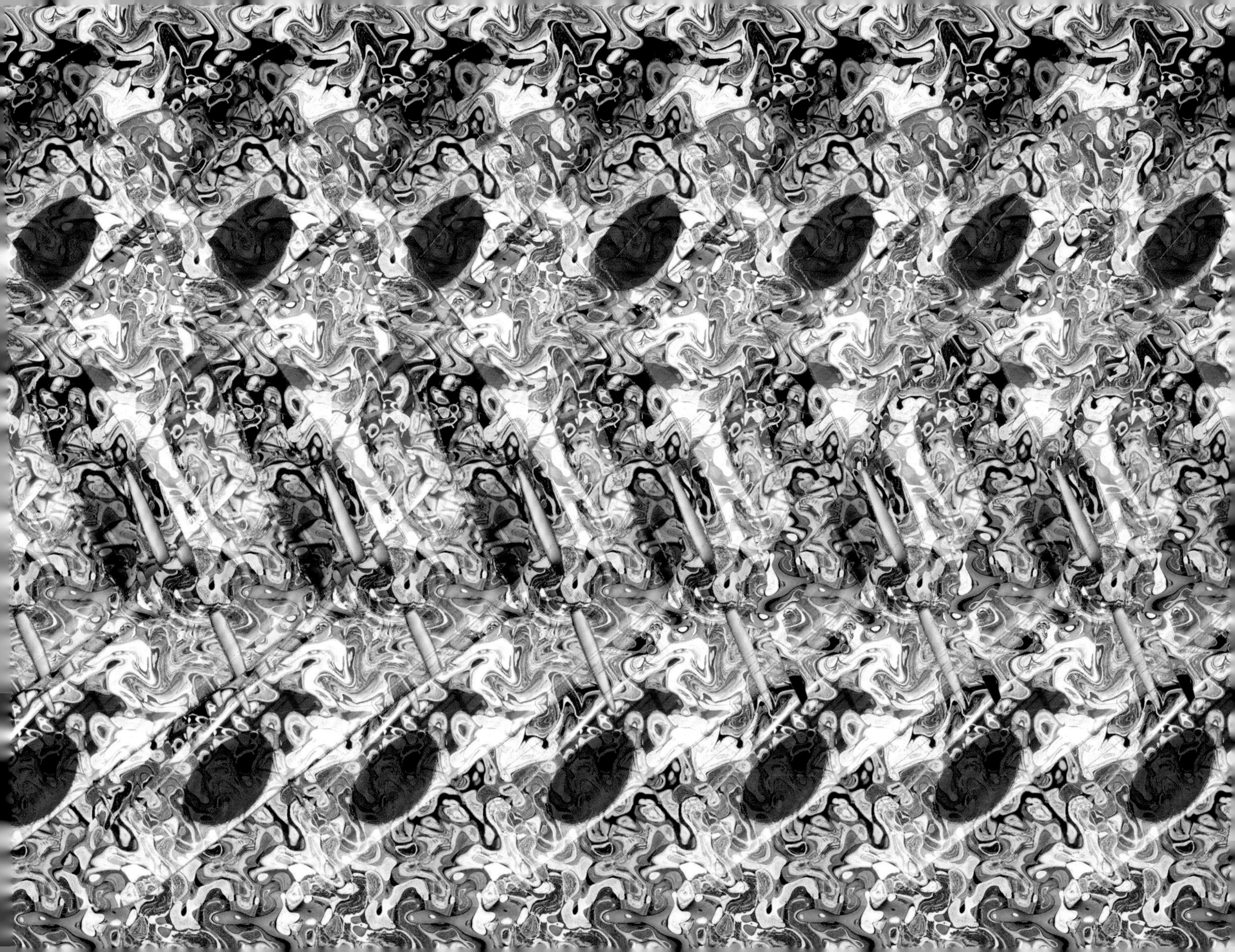

Square Eyes

Stare **at the central** dot, **relax** your eyes, **and watch** as the image comes alive.

Keep **Still!**

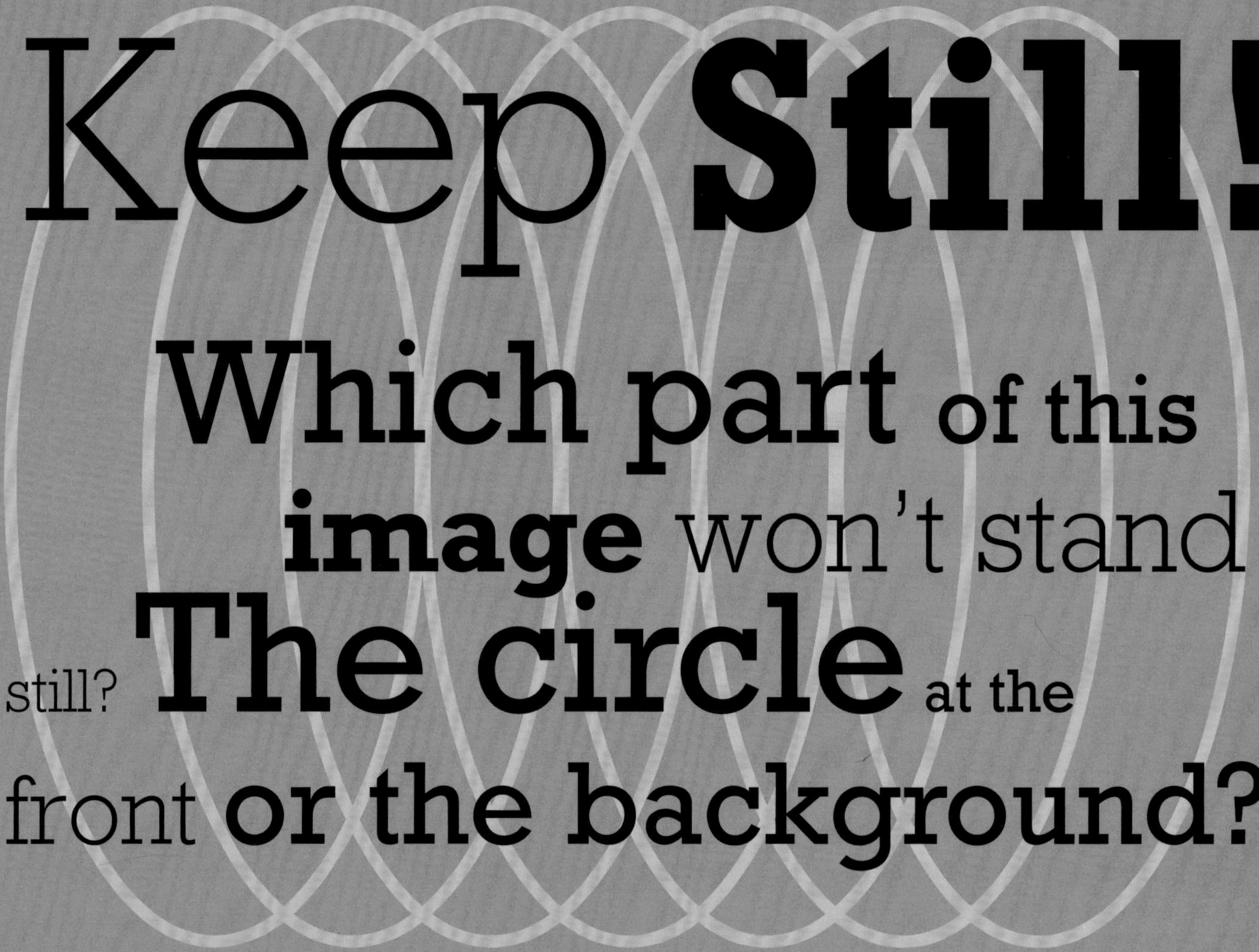

Which part of this image won't stand still? **The circle at the** front **or the background?**

Taking the **Edge Off**

The architect of this **building has got his plans wrong.** The side walls shouldn't still be standing, **but** somehow they are.

Bugs in a BOX

A **looming** hand **lifts** a caterpillar out of a **box— but what's real,** and what's the work **of a** skilled **artist?**

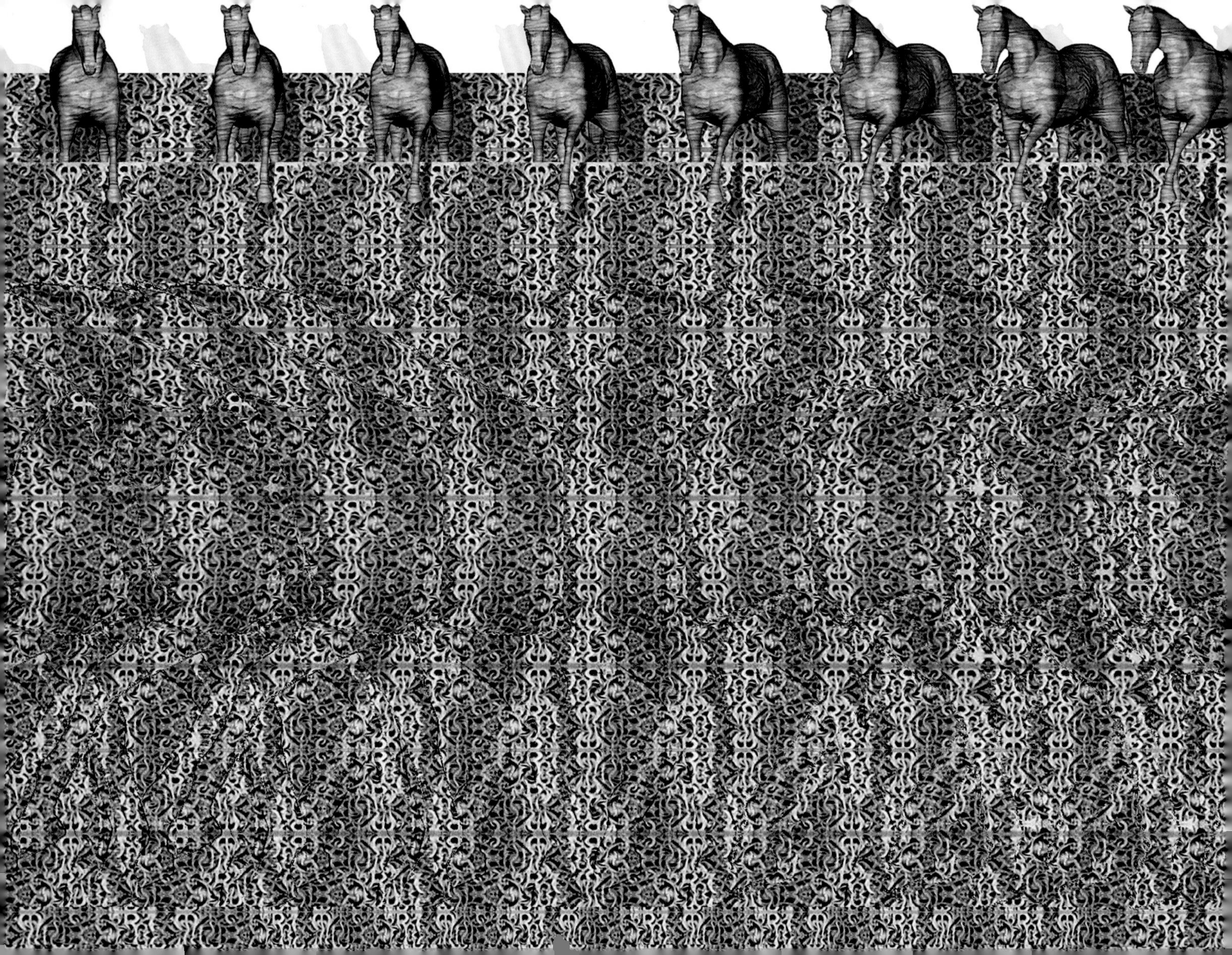

Giddy Up!

Quick, use the **instructions on** page 28 **to see this image before the** horse **gallops away.**

Twister

The spirals coming from the central column in this image move so fast they're making the page vibrate.

Fraser Spiral

Do you see **a spiral...**

or are you actually

looking at **a series of concentric**

circles?

Coffee Break

Which **joker** put jumping beans in the coffee pot?

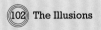

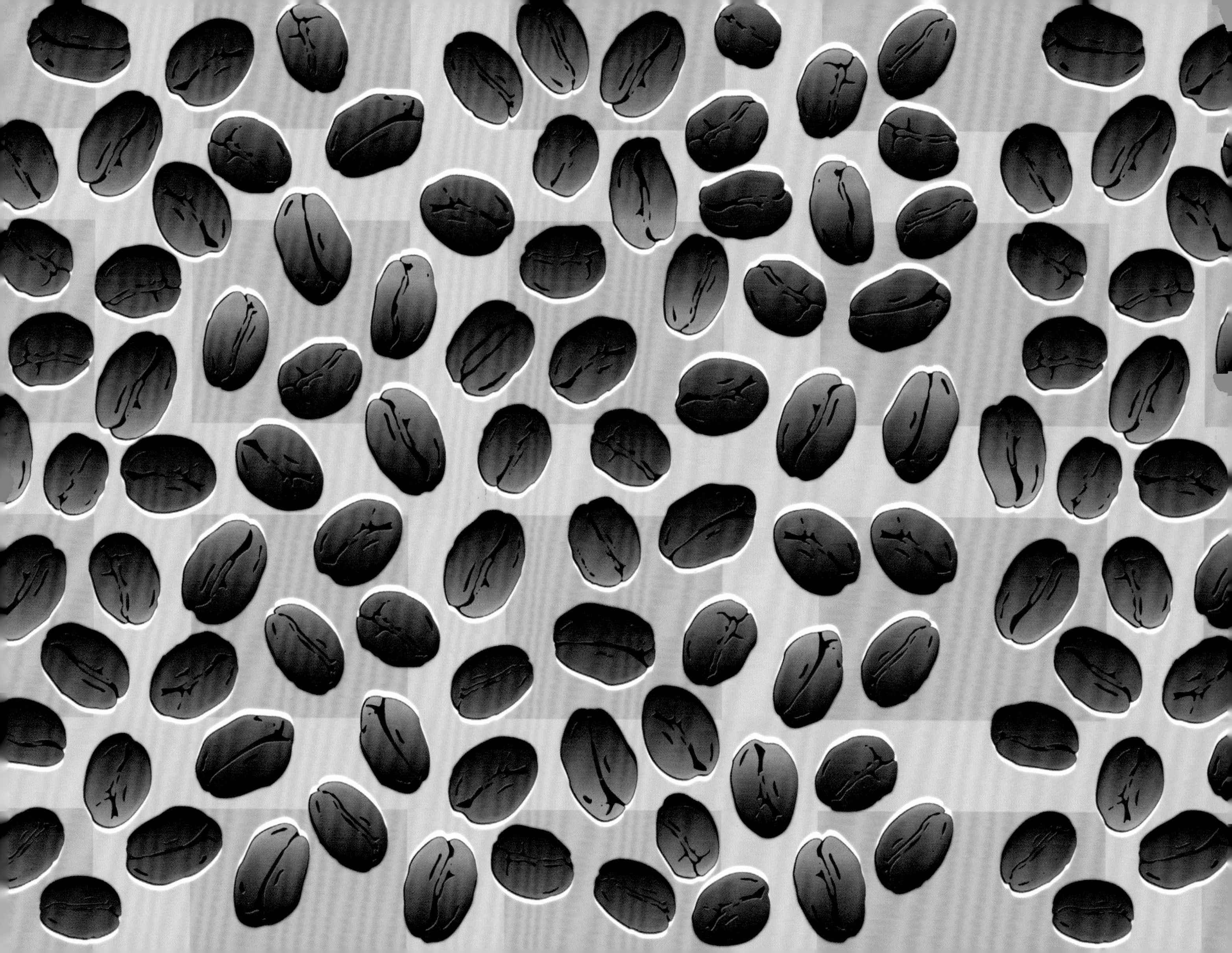

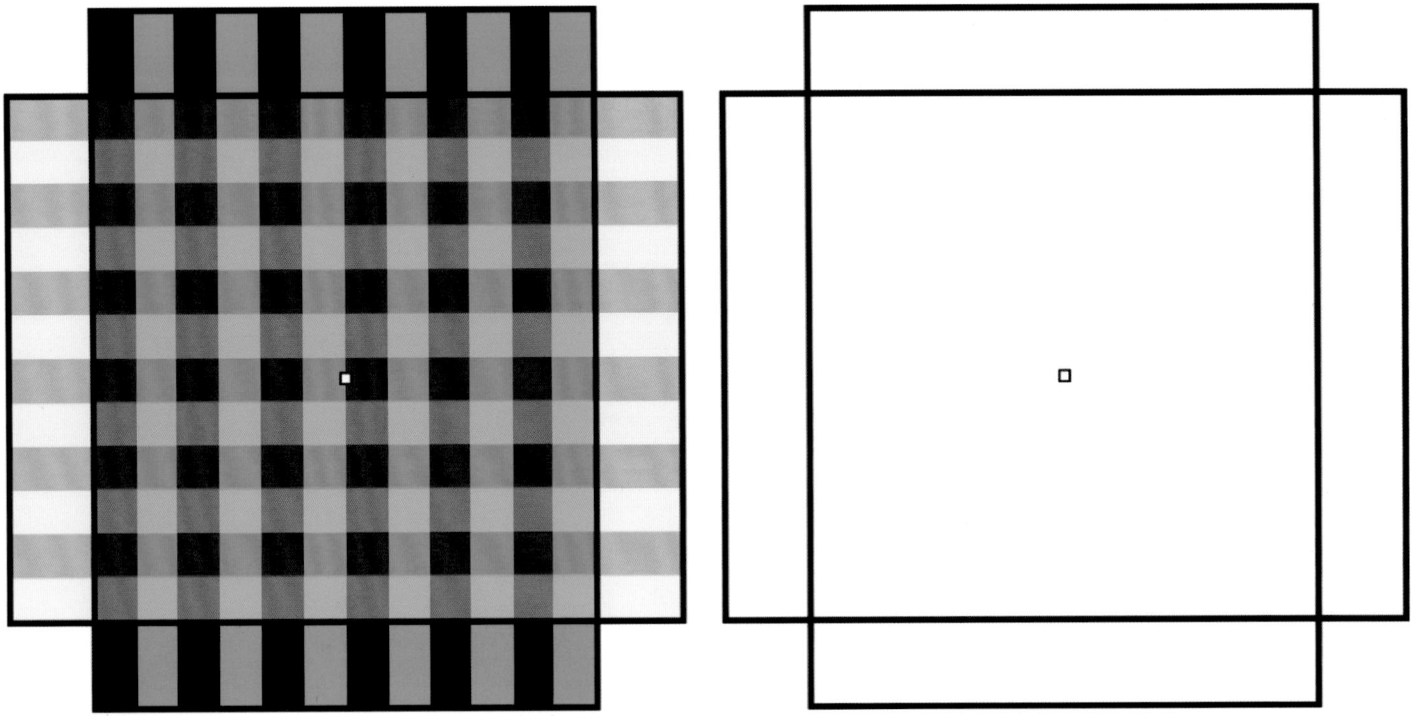

Up, **Down**, Left, **Right**

Does your **brain** predominantly see **horizontal** or **vertical** lines? Stare **at the dot at the center of the lefthand box** for a minute, **then** look at the empty box **next to it** and **all will be** revealed

Hand **Out**

On page 28 you'll find **all the info needed** to reveal who is reaching **out** to **whom.**

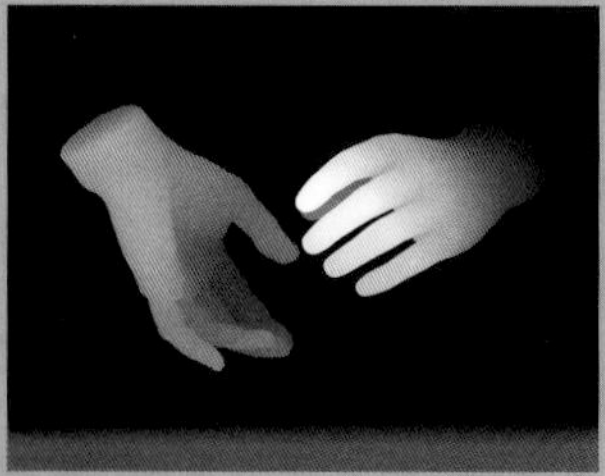

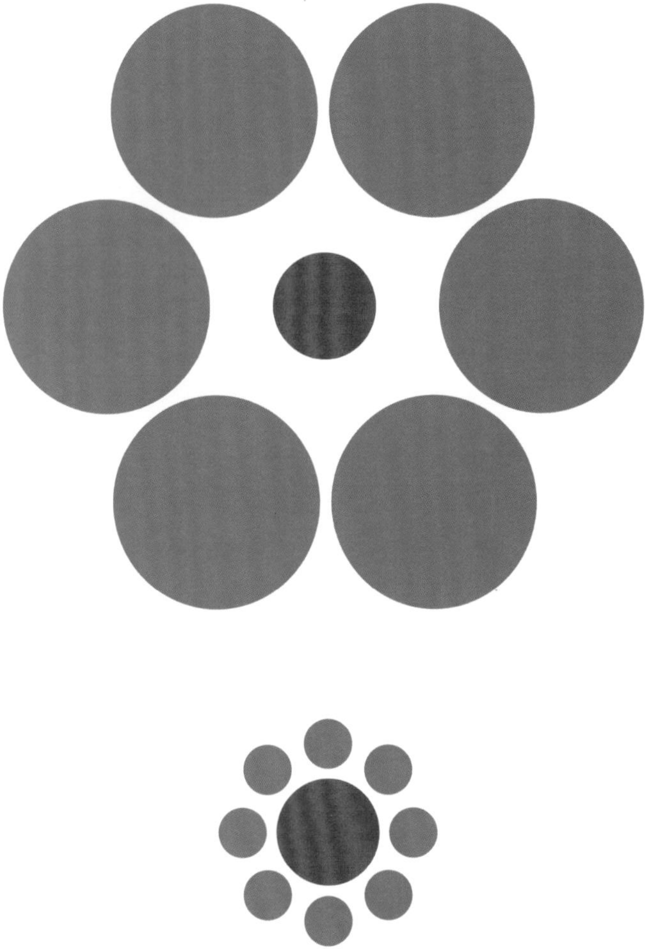

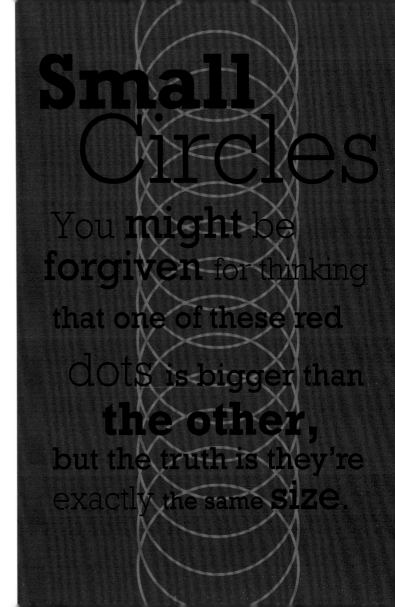

Small Circles

You **might** be **forgiven** for thinking **that one of these red** dots **is bigger than the other,** **but the truth is they're** exactly **the same size.**

Star Fall

Stare at the dot in the middle of the image long enough and the stars will start to disappear.

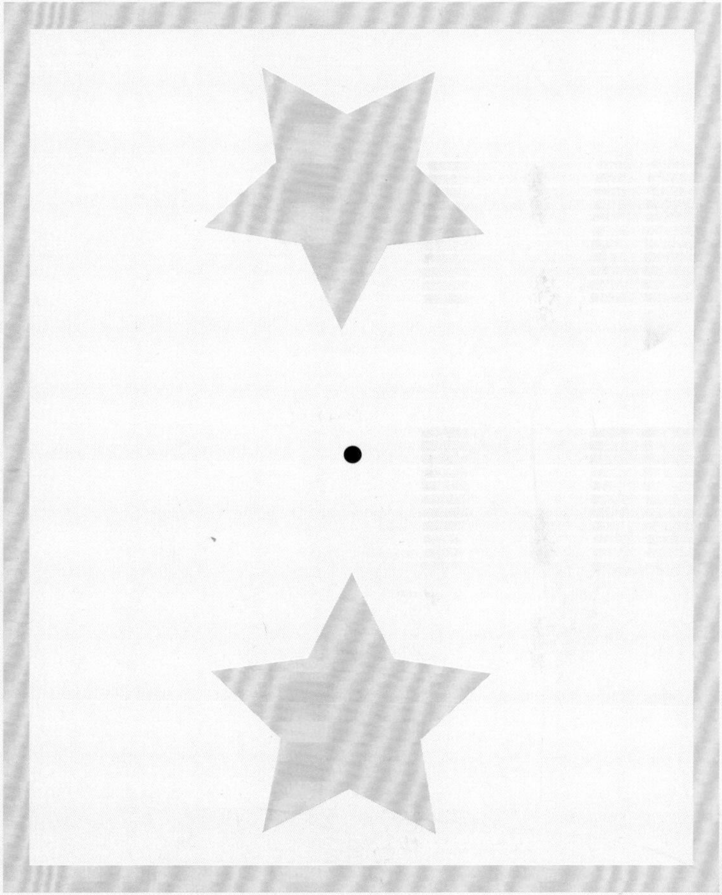

Wavy Checkerboard

The further away you look at this image, the wobblier the lines become.

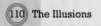

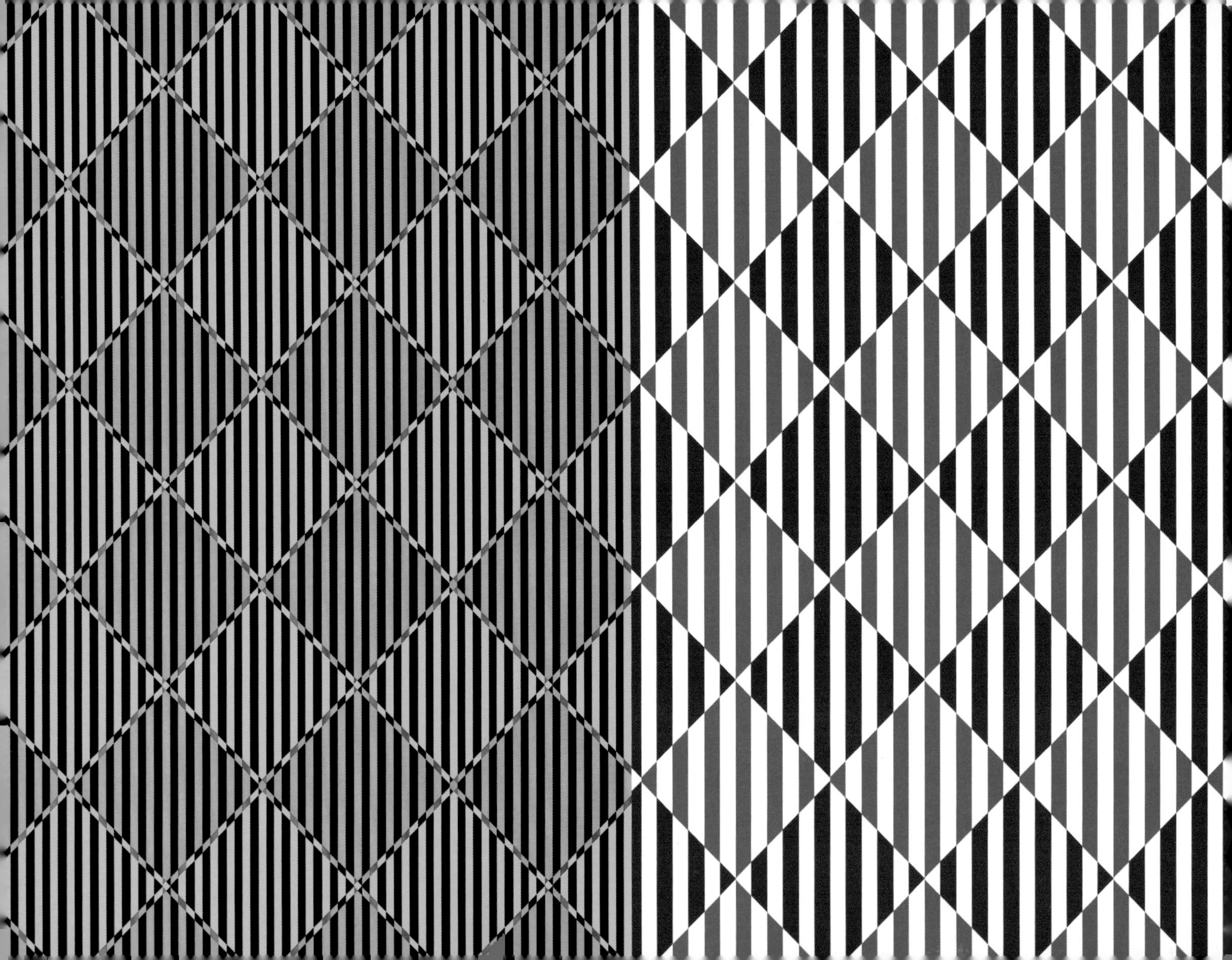

Let's Get This Straight

The lines **between** the diamond shapes look wavy, **but they're actually straight.**

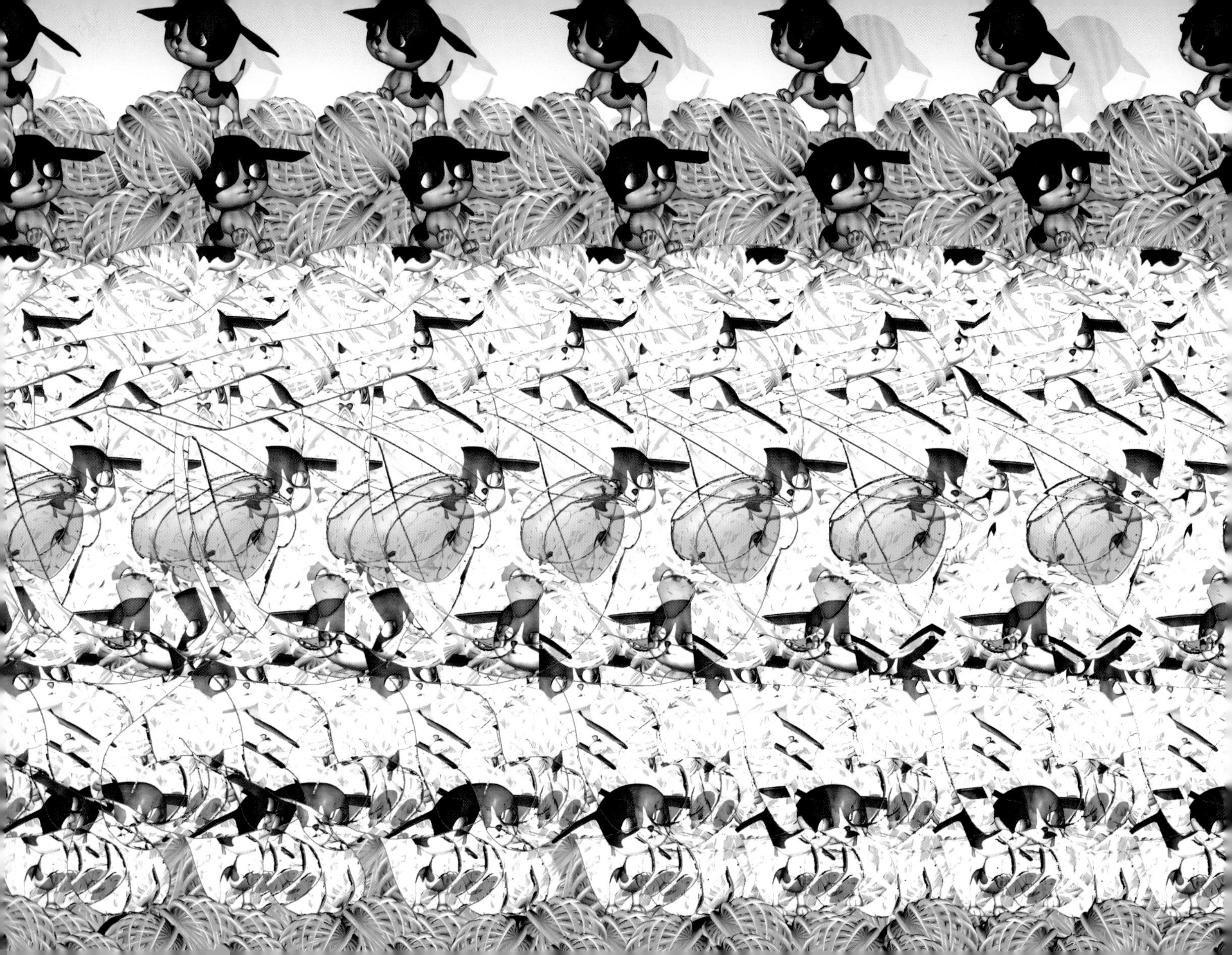

Dog Gone Fun

Can you see this puppy at play? **If not, try following the instructions** on **page 28.**

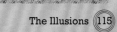

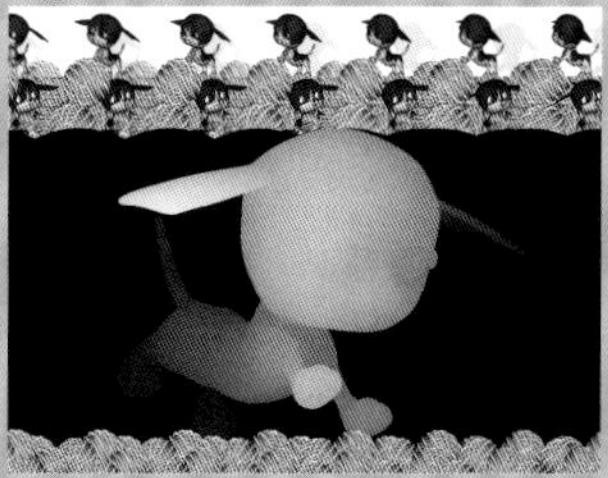

Art Imitates Life

Who's to know where the painted world ends and the real world begins for this artist

No **Escape**

Stuck on a **rooftop path, it seems unlikely that this man will ever find his way to** the door **below.**

Reverse **Opposites**

Who's **upside down** **and** who's right-side up **in this otherwise normal-looking** apartment block?

9
6

Tunnel **Vision**

However hard you **try to escape,** the end **of this tunnel** will forever **remain just out of reach.**

Wood Splitter

This guy doesn't **need an axe.**

Use **the instructions on page 28** to see why.

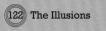

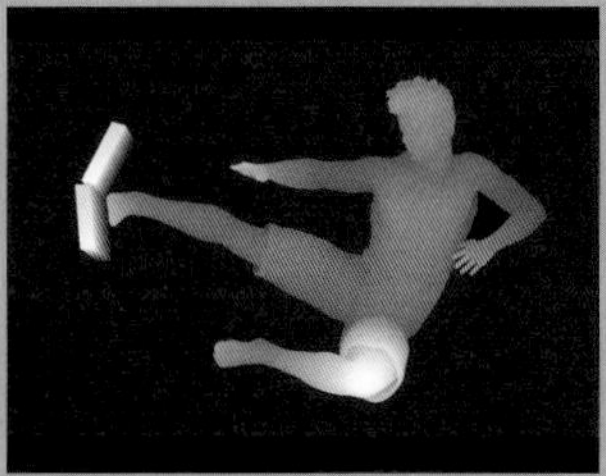

Tangled Star

Which part of this star should come first? **It's impossible to tell.**

Shape Shifting

Can you see **star patterns** or cube shapes? They change all the time!

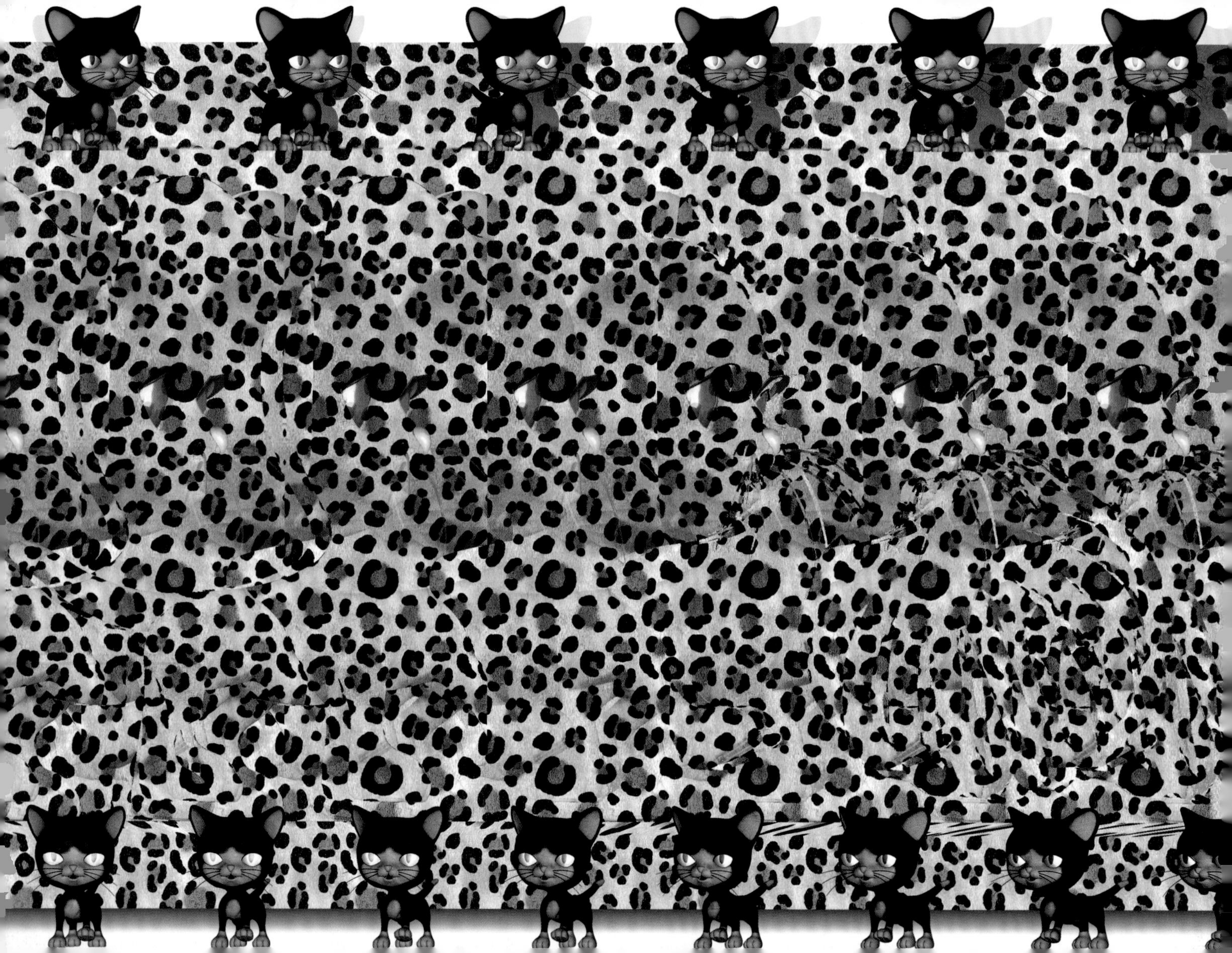

Play Time

Do you see **the kitten** chasing **the ball of wool?** **Get some help** **on page 28** if you can't.

Picture Credits

The publisher would like to thank the below contributors for allowing us to use their amazing images in the book. Please visit their websites and support their work:

Professor Edward H. Adelson page 47

Ciaran Brennan page 24,
www.ciaran-brennan.com

Ramon Bruin pages 70, 95
www.jjkairbrush.nl

Beau Deeley pages 80, 92, 98–99
www.beaudeeley.com

Tom French page 28
www.tomfrenchart.wordpress.com

Erik Johansson pages 82, 116, 117, 118
erikjohanssonphoto.com

Ant Lamb pages 15, 16, 17, 18, 19, 34, 55, 65, 71, 74, 75
www.antlamb.co.uk

Gene Levine pages 65, 72, 89, 96, 107, 114, 123, 126
www.colorstereo.com

David MacDonald page 23
www.cambiguities.com

James Maher page 27
www.jamesmaherphotography.com

Ray Massey pages 66, 67, 79
www.raymassey.com

Joe and Max pages 37, 40, 58
www.3djoeandmax.com

Kaio Nao pages 22, 32, 42–43, 52, 60–61, 85, 120
www.kaianao.com

Simon C Page pages 124, 125
www.simoncpage.co.uk

Planet Streetpainting page 62
www.planetstreetpainting.com

Gianni A. Sarcone pages 20, 44, 48, 49, 76, 103, 112
www.giannisarcone.com

Professor Peter Tse page 104
The image is featured in his book *The Neural Basis of Free Will: Criterial Causation* (MIT Press)

The following images were obtained from Wikipedia and Wikimedia Commons (http://commons.wikimedia.org) using the Creative Commons licence: pages 100, 108, 111

The following photolibrary images were used:
Getty Images: pages 35, 39, 56
iStock: pages 12, 31, 38, 51, 53, 59, 68, 86, 91, 94